THE TALE OF THE HARMATTAN
POEMS

Kraftgriots

Also in the series (POETRY)

THE TALE OF THE HARMATTAN

POEMS

Tanure Ojaide

kraftgriots

Published by

Kraft Books Limited
6A Polytechnic Road, Sango, Ibadan
Box 22084, University of Ibadan Post Office
Ibadan, Oyo State, Nigeria
✆ + 234 (0)803 348 2474, + 234 (0)805 129 1191
E-mail: kraftbooks@yahoo.com
www.kraftbookslimited.com

First published by Kwela Books/Snailpress,
Cape Town, South Africa, 2007
This edition, published by Kraft Books Limited, 2015

ISBN 978–978–918–311–1

= KRAFTGRIOTS =
(A literary imprint of Kraft Books Limited)

First printing, June 2015

Dedication

To:

Hyeladzira Balami for the wonderful days in Maiduguri

In Sundiata's day a griot did not have to fetch water,
To say nothing of farming and gathering firewood.
Father World has changed, changed.

(Banna Kanute's *Sunjata*)

The dream of one man is part of the memory of all.

(Jorge Luis Borges)

Contents

PART I:

OIL REMEDIES

Where is the palm oil red in its aroma that
led spirits by the nose to swim in the bottle?

The goat song

I

I sing the community's goat song.
Folks wear gold over tumours of hope;

they are rounded into a guarded prison
south-south of the mountain palace

where the king and his consorts carouse;
a bacchanalia that breaks the rock of reason.

The capital so afflicted with flatulence,
only thunder can halt insatiable hands

from clearing the commonwealth's table
of cornucopia into paunches of the lords.

Those sitting on wealth are rickety, grovelling
on sand; globules of anguish their only share.

And who cares if foreigners found deep
under their bare feet divine gifts of pools

and started to tap the earth's underbelly
for fuel to blaze brushes of progress?

II

All along wells brought forth rusty colouration;
folks wondered about the sign from beyond –

all along the taste of water from wells exposed
what kind gods held underground for the people;

the gods know best what their devotees know not,
they bless the people with their measures of wealth.

Is health not the greatest wealth? Ask the old
what blessing exceeds the wealth of health.

Must you uncover the wrapped gifts of gods
if you have absolute faith in their benevolence?

I sing the people's goat song –
they wear smiles over deep wounds.

III

They incinerate our dead heroes with flares;
no hardwood for caskets to accord them honour.

Ozidi will not forgive the humiliation.
Ogidigbo will not forgive the insult.

The blackened stream is ancestral blood
tapped away by giant pipes into ships

to rejuvenate foreign cities, invigorate markets;
distant places lit with wonders; here, a blackout.

Agitated, Mowoe flaunts his right forefinger.
In self-defence Saro-Wiwa exhorts foot soldiers.

The wind laments, its fans are burning out;
the trees have been shaved of their coiffures.

The snake is sliding closer to the heart
and its venom intensifies with every strike.

The big family is dying out – irokos fall; game
leave in droves, and humans flee to hunger.

Soon the whole landscape will be a cemetery
south-south of the carousing palace of the king.

The carrion lord cares not for the rot he stirs;
he pranks with consorts in the death-field –

Government and the coalition of global lords
have snatched away what ancestors sat upon.

I sing the land's goat song;
the last cry of its warriors.

Priests, converts, and gods

Pentecostal converts burnt down the primeval grove –
there, they believed, witches metamorphosed into owls;

they did not even know what animals they had become,
when they were *born again*, living in self-renunciation.

The developers tore down the forest that covered us
with green foliage, trashed the natural canopies –

they argued we needed roads to go out, as if we knew
nothing of adventure or did not visit other places.

They also argued we needed schools and football fields,
not to continue living in the bush where they found us.

It was futile explaining to them the divine splendour
when the archer sun shoots gold-tinted arrows between leaves;

it was a shame that those who loved colours didn't see
the spectacle of rain, wearing reeds, perform a stilt dance.

After school I looked out for the public park,
the community of plants and animals, they promised

but they only felled more trees for cemeteries, forbade burials
in homes to confine ghosts to fenced lots and make towns safe.

Worshipping a foreign-accented god, they thrust a blazing firebrand
at the behind of the war-god who fled his guard without looking back.

Up north the Sahara devouring plants advances ferociously
after gulping the River Niger in a generation-long fit of thirst.

In the south campfires of oil barons litter the landscape;
stoked all year round by helmet-wearing graduates

who consider themselves lucky, paid foreign currency
instead of the naira; an astute ploy to buy their loyalty.

The streams and creeks clogged to keep ocean tankers full,
we no more boast of fresh water or the abundance of fish

We know the capital gain from the blessed but besieged land
will go down the drain for a caste to maintain its smug smile.

The priests that came from abroad warned of the inferno
that would consume those who did not heed their commandments –

they were wrong in attributing hell to another life; it is
here victims already suffer daily pangs from profiteers,

condemned to burning winds of gas flares and streams
of boiling oil so combustible they burn all in their wake.

Dots within a circle

1
Crocodiles lose patience under sustained attack.

2
Boats make bonfires for depressed fishermen.

3
The lingua franca of green lost its alphabet to poachers.

4
Cadavers and ailing captives – all that's left of the record fleet.

5
Rain is the heavenly Niger with open floodgates.

6
A mute parrot amidst blaring flares.

7
Neither rising nor setting: the sun consumed by flames.

8
Water suffers fatally from smudges of human excess.

9
Loud prayers muffle birds singing of dawn.

Womb-wrapped

1

From the original womb, one comes out
crying hysterically at the boundless bounty.

2

In the forest birdsong after birdsong leads
the minstrel into the muse's ample bosom.

3

When the minstrel sang out loud, he beheld
a crowd; a cloud of talkative birds his chorus.

4

The minstrel is the land's rooster –
he ushers in dawn with a trumpet.

5

The boat is bringing from the sea a beauty
with her mirrors and powder; the minstrel awestruck.

6

The storm picked the sea's spirit to litter here –
in her bed of coral, Mami Wata smiles to herself.

7

As I dip feet and hands into the herb-dark stream
of my birth, I hear oil blowouts closer and closer.

8

Let me stand in the shadow of the iroko
before next season's lightning strikes it.

9

The stream shrinks and stands still
at the sight of a snaking oil slick.

10

On either side drum-carving trees –
I hear heart-throbs; mortal fear of fire.

11

The young fisherman caught cowries in his net –
his priesthood in later years pre-ordained.

12

The fuming forest forages for light;
every step ambushed by sand dunes.

13

Wearing Shell-coated gear,
the arsonist escapes finger-printing.

Quatrain suite

1

To have loved Mami Wata in her underwater palace of coral:
to have had trysts with the moon in her days of full glory,
to have tasted one dish and never wished for another,
and to have lived here when it was a different country!

2

My memories chase out the army of poachers.
In their green outfit of old seasons they restore
the tattered map of the country. Now the starving
amongst us trip over carcasses they won't even touch.

3

I look for the reed in the tide, the resilient spirit
bending but never breaking; the slim one
that relishes its God-given supple limbs –
now another casualty drowned in oil slush.

4

Before the fisherman could finish building a boat to evacuate,
the river dried up and horses galloped through to capture him –
in exile he remembered the moats of Benin did not stop swarms of locusts
from devastating the city and having their fill of blood and bronze.

5

The map of my homeland has changed.
The cartographers blot out forests and rivers.
Oil wells and flares dot the new landscape –
now nobody recognizes the beauty queen's face.

6

The primeval inhabitants of the land
suffer martyrdom at the hands of poachers

who blast them out of their naïve existence.
The Niger loses draughts; memories of majesty.

7

For good luck I carry about memories of floodwater,
primarily the seven-day storm that sank sun and moon
in gurgling streams and creeks, the entire land a seascape
when my bait-free new hooks caught catfish and mudfish.

8

The apiapia cries hysterically, flying over its former haunt:
"It's another planting season and what a cheerless sight,
hardly any farmers!" They fled to be servants in the city.
Who blames bird or migrant, the soil one barren crust?

9

Evergreens bald, every head bowed in disgrace.
No season grows back flared or suffocated leaves
and the cycle of self-succeeding generations dies.
Green is now a scarce commodity in the rain forest.

10

The eye of the earth beholds a vandalized fortune.
The ears of the earth numb from the deep silence.
Its veins clogged by an abundance of oily grease,
its heart beats an irregular drum that fades away.

11

When wood copulates with iron,
the axe is born and groomed
to chop down more trees.
Suicide goes by many names.

12

The iroko knows not how it can survive the iron era
to welcome eagles to its crown. I wish I knew how.
Globalization is a category-5 hurricane; its direction

escapes forecast – it leaves litters in an insane trail.

13

We have plenty of bait but no fish in the water –
decades of genocide, millions of victims.
Once earthworms begin to consume themselves,
the world would've run its cycle; a predator's paradise.

14

The rich among us used to boast of the many barrels
of palm oil they produced in the season of industry.
Then came spills and flares that burnt out palm trees.
Today the government and Shell toast their oil fortune.

15

The birds and beetles lost their refuge, as people
of the creeks lost their sun, moon, and stars to fumes.
Why are survivors of the globalization assault only
the insignia of commanders-in-chief, vultures and cobras?

16

When the migrant birds return, how will they know
their homes from others in the wilted dominion?
If they stray from the native soil, it's because
flaring winds blew them to where nobody lives.

17

In town there are new roads and signposts
as well as waves of rats and migrants –
democracy demolished monuments of dictators
for good, but still we bleed . .

Lessons from grandma's night-time school

I

I used to throw up a copper coin for head
or tail; it was a simple choice I wanted to make –

it used to be easy to make up one's mind,
as head or tail belonged to the same disk.

Because we have lost respect for basic things,
there is no coin left in a democracy's dividends

and confusion paralyses the mind's every move.
Up or down, right or left, blurred direction.

II

The Omoja was too shallow to follow to the sea;
when rafts barely made it deep, I took to boats

and so fished the bigger streams singing to Mami Wata
to bring me boatloads of good fortune from far depths.

We cast nets wide for the turtle of the tales
to torment the trickster in a boiling cauldron.

III

We were great boys everywhere,
took giant strides in daydreams;

crossed bridges suspended from tall wishes
into landscapes without dust without death.

We wore dirt without rashes, had no fear
of dying though we feared seeings corpses.

Every season fêted residents with abundance
and we reciprocated hospitality with offerings;

rites that moved from one grade to another
and made graduates proud of their learning.

Humans and spirits married for love of life;
spouses eschewed insults and court cases.

We reaped bushels of goodwill without effort
because no-one ate outside the open gathering –

a morsel multiplied into meals
to sate a thousand stomachs.

We consorted with birds and animals,
communed with plants on fresh draughts

that rain and sunlight provided for growth;
no cause for anxiety in the commonwealth.

For my grandchild

My children have had no scholarships;
they can't fish or tap rubber as I once did,

the river transformed into a snake of a tomb
and the forest fraught with flares and fumes.

With crude oil gushing into slave ships
refurbished as free-market super-tankers,

the government assures people of development
with proceeds from export and spot market deals.

No jobs for the graduates in the oil sector
even as wells litter the family's farmlands.

In the daily dearth of prospects staring at all,
mobile policemen brandish guns in the sun

and, from a safe distance above the ground,
hired retired marines keep the pipelines safe.

Villages of imploring eyes marching, hands up-
raised with green-leafed branches, mowed down.

CNN & BBC embedded with Chevron and Shell
report that local women, stripping before cameras

to save their dying children and men, are primitive.
In their secure wings they know not Ogoni's agonies.

With my grandchild born, the new Stone Age
of a nation very black in the books has begun

with refilled slave ships refurbished as super-tankers
anchored at Escravos and poaching inland as centuries ago.

Tale of the harmattan

It is harmattan, time to prepare every hearth
to combat northeast winds, fierce warriors

that this year have lost their frostbite
but still stir swirls of inescapable dust.

They say in their home country the dunes
have never enjoyed such massive fortune.

On the way hosts slashed and burnt trees
for the desert to advance without hindrance.

Season of brush fires, kites fly overhead
in festive formations in smoke-smothered skies;

still we lose not thatched homes or barns
since we keep a wide buffer state, a clearing.

The season's blaze diminishes the hard labour
demanded in preparation for the next planting.

But this season's like no other in the minstrel's memory;
the rubber tappers are frustrated with anaemic trees

suffering hardship and baldness from a neighbouring
business that devours whatever stands before it.

The exciting spirit of the harmattan is lost on us,
there is nothing to celebrate with bonfires

because the regular visitor failed to arrive
with the good luck that follows its wake –

the swarm of generous djinns that invade us
barred from the land by free marketers of oil.

In place of heat from the log-stoked hearth,
we burn from gas flares and oil blowouts

on insomniac nights in the big compound.
We no longer swathe ourselves from cold

in one blanket, warm and inhaling body odour;
the sparkling hearth telling our tale of the harmattan.

Market day

Day of anticipation, day of give-and-take;
day that lights the community as one flame

welcomes strangers to our midst, welcomes
even our dead now costumed in alien habits.

On market eves spirits hold a large fair
to prepare for daylight display of wares.

In this market I can no longer get my needs,
the same market that filled my forebears.

Where is the home-grown bean dish that sat
living, dead, and tortoise to consort with greed?

Where is the palm oil red in its aroma that
led spirits by the nose to swim in the bottle?

Where is the outlay of fabrics from home cotton
that costumed the chameleon chieftain of fashion?

O market god, conjurer god of the milling place,
god of colours, god of flavours and the handmade,

fill the market with the items that tales passed to us
but we now find beyond our means in distant places:

snails men shunned as women's food till they tasted
the delicacy and always asked for them to round up;

porcupine meat that bristles covered till cooked
for the salivating mouth to devour in banga soup!

Fresh fish that with lemon leaves for dinner cut short
children's play outside before elders consumed all,

yams and beans that knocked out every adult and
laid them flat to daydream in a world that is gone;

cherries and mangoes earned children their first coins;
left them constipated from leftovers of their secret feast . . .

O god of gathering places, watchful but distracted eye,
sever yourself from new gods that cut you down

from pre-eminent status to a wandering beggar.
Are you not the fabled spirit of abundance?

Welcome strangers as always – they enrich us –
but take out poachers, arsonists, and robbers;

bring back produce and products of our hands;
fill sheds with what stories credit you with pride:

what the soil brings forth through tendering,
the game and fish that sustain healthy ones.

Let all the cardinal points bring buyers and sellers,
let nearby and distant ones come to marvel

at the original wealth, the song of abundance:
a collision of colours, the spectacle of good life . . .

Oil remedies

Produce of the blessed palm tree, testimony
of industry of men and women; oil confers wealth.

Rules kept trees safe from avid cutlasses.
Elixir in the people's home, oil sustains life.

We knew our brides by the lavish oil
that massaged their bodies to glow with allure –

preserver of skin from cracking harmattan,
there is oil in the bride's praise repertory.

Oil is the lamp we keep at the crossroads
for humans and spirits to find separate ways.

A decongestant relieving patients of acute cough,
priceless oil the ointment that heals wounds –

necessity of every household and homestead,
it dispenses health in the clinic-less community.

The same oil that makes every meal a feast
for the palate and completes every rich dish!

In searches in the dark it fuels the firebrand
that clears the way for passage to safety.

The oil we know has always been the lamp –
friend of the eyes, it fuels a bright spectacle.

Then came subsoil oil, no longer red but black,
converted by entrepreneurs into capital fuel.

This oil bleeding from the earth flowers light
and they sing hymns to fan its incandescence.

It is we who live in the dark that give out light.
They make bonfires of our blind ancestors' gifts

after hauling away priceless pools of abundance
and leaving with us silent and roaming epidemics.

Warri has never really been a beauty

I

In the rubble a dirge assaults the minstrel.
Staring at him the blackened face of walls,

remains of storefronts; shadows dead on their feet.
Quarters disembowelled to plant weeds in dirt.

Ghosts want to embrace the minstrel in the street
where fugitives shed liveries for permanent rest.

There flowers fall from heartless sorties –
to every breast a sad thorn to wear to bed.

It is not right for birds to lose their voices at dawn;
it is not customary to rifle feathers for grenades,

but Warri and its environs groan from bad blood –
weeds take over; the moon a cemetery of sunflowers.

Now the military arrest and humiliate passers-by,
hands upraised in surrender to harsh blackmail.

But tell me where in town the song is not sad,
where sunbirds cohabit with flowering plants?

At night the moon elegant in white linen
offers lovers outdoors to lift the heart

and on the riverbanks a curfew doesn't curtail
the heaving breasts of waves, warm to embrace.

All share the sun, clouds, and rain without squabbling;
the breeze buys no argument of ethnicity and cools all.

Tomorrow will ferry them through deep night
on its raft to the dawn that their prayers plead for.

There are hungry ones on either side of the divide
and the Red Cross crosses the line to give out loaves.

Warri is saturated with prayers and dearth of goodwill
but guns will neither repay the debt nor clean the dirt.

II

Warri has never really been a beauty
but this defaced figure is not my love.

At 10 Radio Road I vacationed cheerfully
after bidding village home goodbye.

Federal Government College thrilled –
there's been no citadel as filled with joy;

there every group came together as one;
there was love in everybody's heart.

Now there are two parallel roads with multiple
turns – when you are in one turn you are Urhobo;

in another you are Itsekiri, and yet another Izon,
and can't escape being cornered into ethnic bunkers.

But enter one of those false fortifications
and fire and smoke will drive you out –

there's so much pepper blown into eyes
you will be hounded out by head-hunters.

There are bridges to cross to safe ground
but they ferry families under at night –

where they go towards the sea is death,
where they flee to inland is also death

and they evacuate the town of all tongues
to join separate militias and be damned.

Warri has never really been a beauty
but this defaced figure is not my love.

PART II:

AT THE KAIAMA BRIDGE

Those who bring a running fight to the iguana
will lose their breath and withdraw before long.

At the kaiama bridge

I see them retreat, flotillas of river spirits
who for centuries brought their spectacle to town
in yearly masquerades – they retreat seaward.
What becomes of us without their presence?

Along in the southward flow, all other water-
born names, once guests on land, return –
they are no longer safe in the drilling wetlands
that from beginning hosted the congress of life.

All with the property of land gone into water
to relieve themselves of the scathing noise above
return to the hard soil posthaste because now
the waters have turned to a poisonous brew.

We have organized a resistance army,
declared sovereignty over our resources;
but have not pushed back the poachers.
Outside forces pillage the inheritance.

I see the oil-blackened current suffocating
Mami Wata and her retinue of water-maids;
they leave fast the inhospitable dominion
for the freedom and health of the open sea.

I have not seen a regatta in three decades.
Nor have I seen the island's boat of songs
raise its ritual paddle in salute to high gods
that astronauts now suffocate with satellites.

Oil spillage has fuelled water hyacinths
to multiply astronomically across rivers.
Refugee gods are taking the last route
before the entire waterway is clogged.

Neighbours are surrendering their homes
to destruction by the fires from above.
Others have the soil burning underfoot,
their shield of green gone; mere ashes.

The refugees are removed from the fields
in company buses, a humanitarian gesture;
then in diarrhoea-infected camps force-fed
genetically modified corn meant for cows.

Do I want to shed blood defending the wealth
that the gods themselves have given up
because they know in their serene silence
the barbaric charge of godless ones after them?

Is revolution dead and must the Egbesu Boys
surrender rights of ownership and humanity
to the brigand lord and his fierce livery
of insatiable appetites raising a flaming flag?

At the wobbling Kaiama Bridge that holds the Delta
together, I see a procession of oil-soaked water spirits
wailing their way out. No boats of fishermen plying
the waterways; no regatta and no swimmers in sight.

The fortune

Where the creeks enter the sea
Olokun filled me a boat to keep.

It was left for me to take home
without crying for more help

through pirates betting their lives
on unescorted cargoes passing –

robbers keep mirrors in closets
to foresee the fortune of others.

I steered upstream as I must;
the boat mine to take home

but it was too large and loaded
for the creeks that took me home –

the fingers of the Niger did not
always reach everywhere nearby.

At the last deep water station,
destitute hands waited to off-load

the cargo and be head carriers
for the rest of the shallow way.

No road for boats to my home,
only logs floated there in floods –

the sky turned off its sprinklers
and rafters sat at home, waiting.

Among my helpers pilfering ones
that I can't convert into clean souls.

My home is large but not loaded
though Olokun filled me a boat.

Swimming in a waterhole

We grew up to love rivers and lakes, open refuge
that saved children from the hard labour at home –

every parent knew where first to look for a missing child
before ever alerting the town-crier to beat the drum.

Many of us did not concentrate at school in anticipation
of going straight to swim until dusk when eyes turned red.

Rivers and lakes must have cried themselves into silence –
we spent nothing of our millions of earnings to save them.

For decades water hyacinth overran the pristine waterscape
in convoys of weed and started stifling the beautiful host.

With the oil companies only looking after profit margins,
oil slicks easily found their way to bury the waters alive.

Parents still make demands of children as never before;
the ageless sun remains master archer in the dry season

and young ones ever restless seek new bathing spots
to relieve themselves of the sun's scorching gaze.

Burrow pits of road builders, deluged into perennial
waterholes, provide respite from hard labour at home

but there no fish, no water spirits borne by currents;
no Mami Wata and others to share the salt of life.

In these holes abandoned caterpillars and other monsters
drag down the swimmer without recourse to a treat.

We are fortunate we still swim in groups in the open.
After gas flares, oil slicks, and hyacinths converge

to turn rain into acid and all the methane seeps in
to raise new syndromes that destroy the body,

where next to seek refuge from step-mothers
when the sun flares up in its sadistic fit?

Without the trees

Without the trees
the wind no longer gestures playfully to me

without the evergreens
nobody speaks the lingua franca to me

without the creeks
the rains no longer sate my voracious appetite

without the currents
the flying-fish no longer makes sorties into my soup pot

without the sun (now fumigated)
the sunbird no longer plays patiently with me

without the shrubs (already devoured by fire)
the dew no longer delivers to me the message of dawn

without the forest (now poached to death)
the choral ensemble of hyrax, woodpecker & co. no longer
performs for me

without the farms
the butterflies no longer indulge me with a colourful pageant

without the stars (all smothered)
I nightly lose my way to the congress with ancestors.

Transplants

I see transplants of my youth's landscape
first at Hawthornden and now at Steepletop:

the pristine streams, the multiethnic population
of plants, costumed birds, and graceful game.

Surely no bears, coyotes, or foxes there
but deer, antelope, and porcupine dazzle.

Birch, eucalyptus, maple, and pine are
older than me – their barks recount centuries of seasons.

Iroko and mahogany are hardly seen; the forest fell
foul to fires of oil blowouts and poaching raids.

These streams still flow as they did centuries ago;
the creeks I fished in without care now clogged.

This orange dusk on a forest trail with colleagues
brought home Godwin, Boyi, and Obatavwe –

we no longer have a place to meet, chased from
home into Warri and Port Harcourt to seek jobs.

At early dawn I will break dew on a trail; mere exercise –
not with Grandma Amreghe to the farm, long planted.

In a half-century one world disappeared; another persists.
Only outside do I now see the landscape of my childhood.

(August 13, 2004)

For the egbesu boys

With your white headband the god you serve
recognizes your steadfast faith in his power –

Egbesu retreats not from a war thrust upon him!
Supreme warrior, Egbesu runs not from a fight.

Let the overlords call you obscene names.
Let the benefactors of robbers vilify you.

Let favourites of tyrants harass you without rest,
let criminals and outlaws call you callous names;

let their cohorts aim guns and grenades at you,
let them burn your villages and green refuge –

the state lord and his mercenary army
stand guilty of crimes against humanity.

As for their individual or corporate end,
let the minstrel not speculate their hell.

Who breaks into your home to kill you
draws from you all means of self-defence;

who trespasses into your inherited land
draws the wrath of your ancestors and gods.

What are offspring that cannot keep their heritage;
what are devotees that cannot protect their faith?

Who comes to your home to rape your bride
tests your courage before the vile act –

what man cannot cover his love with his body
deserves a shameful appellation, nothing better.

I call on you, Egbesu, marshal of the mangroves,
acclaimed war-god of born fishers and farmers,

to stand steadfast behind your great boys –
true devotees ready to be martyred for you.

For the same reason I sang praises of Ogoni youths,
I praise you Egbesu Boys in song – you cannot be

shackled from enjoying your own land's blessings;
you do the honourable duty of brave sons – fight on.

I, devotee of Ivwri, colleague of your Ifri, sing this.
Egbesu, I invoke your warrior spirit for the boys

to triumph over multiple cavalries of capital forces,
triumph over those come to throw them out of home.

Egbesu Boys, dismiss with your blood the charge
of robbery by the coalition of global powers.

You cannot live on your rivers, primeval providers;
they kill the fish population with a sludge of poisons.

You cannot even drink water from anywhere –
they pissed down barrels of arsenic into it.

They flare gas to raise demands for the commodity
and in so doing mangle every farmer's harvest;

they spray the airspace with methanol and insidious
chemicals – you cannot breathe clean air anymore

with the particulate matter of fumes breeding
an asthmatic and cancer-prone generation.

They set hunger on the loose after you;
they unleashed diseases to devour you.

And do they expect you to sit and be enslaved?
Do they expect you to die without fighting back?

Those who bring a running fight to the iguana
will lose their breath and withdraw before long –

the poaching army will stop by the waterside;
the Navy cannot penetrate the fingers of the Niger

and those who know their land from birth
cannot be pushed out by armed invaders

because they have the ultimate weapons
that frustrate the occupying armada –

history is replete with withdrawing troops
of occupiers; shame and death await them.

And so the amphibian forces of young and old,
men and women, hold their own defying threats.

True sons you are, Egbesu Boys, to come
in front to cover your people from death;

true devotees, you have shown deep faith
and Egbesu arms you with an arsenal of justice

that will always triumph in the prolonged battle.
Justice is invincible and robbers will be routed

despite massive superpower arms they import
and multiple billions they commit against justice.

One should not fear death and become a slave
because slavery deprives one of life itself;

one cannot live giving up to another what
makes one's life. That is no life, without life.

When they bring a fight to you in your home,
let them come over your body to take yours!

Dialogue

Delta:

A dozen nations and a hundred tongues
serenade you dusk to dawn and daylong.

Niger:

Farmers and fishers chant you praises
to bring down the sky's tears every season.

Delta:

No longer the seniority of the mountain source,
since from the same earth we rise and fall.

Niger:

Nor of the sea in the life of the river;
both are waters, coevals of the earth.

Delta:

Your course of majesty blazes the soil.

Niger:

Your boundless wetlands sustain lives.

Delta:

The feet that stand the head upright
have rightful claim to its revered height.

Niger:

I cannot bring back my youth from the Futa Djalon;
hunched at Djenné, I must stretch my feet seaward.

Delta:

I am deep to the neck in mud, trampled
by the green foliage that is my robe.

Niger:

Is there a flag without flaring colours?
My name is your shield!

Delta:

My shield more than sustains you!
My name is only complete after yours.

Niger:

This reciprocity springs from both.
We come to each other halfway.

Delta:

My bosom gives you the energy to live
despite your complicity with inland lords.

Niger:

What child is older than its parent?
You cannot live without me.
Row the boat to the sea.
Fast and fast, row the boat.

Delta:

The boat always passes here to the sea.
What course stronger than this current
in hundreds of draughts can drown
the vast calabash that is my dear life?

PART III:

OTHER POEMS

The ancestors are findings it hard to surrender
the game that for ages was the clan's totem.

The rains come

The rains come with fresh rumours –
they mirror the people's horror
at gods that pour scorn on worshippers.

The rains come with a spring of surprises –
the rainmakers drown in their forecasts;
the fishers catch bones in their nets.

The rains fall to tell tall tales to their hosts –
where they come from there is no water, but
on their way they rob moisture to dump here.

The rains come with faith in superstitions –
if they fall hard, believe it, they sob drums;
renowned rainmakers know not how to swim.

The rains come wearing dust all over
only to be groomed and brocaded green
and be paraded brides of all seasons.

The rains come with tales of magic –
they come, thirsty nomads, dying from
starvation and gods' tears sate them.

The rains come trembling on stilts
of reeds that bend but do not break;
they fall on their feet but never prostrate.

The rains come to an evacuated state
to establish a dominion of lavish life
and stay for a season of abundance;

the rains come from somewhere
that cares to assuage others' needs,
bring life to spirit and spirit to life.

The rains come with lessons –
one complements the other;
none complete without another

The wind is blowing my mind away

I

The wind is blowing my mind away.
I hold on to the clothesline in my yard.

A town young with grey hair is passing.
I nod my head but cannot open my mouth

to say what startles me from daydream.
I am tongue-tied in the midst of parrots.

The nose smells a banquet of flavours
that won't get to everyone who wants.

The eyes shine but can't see far
through the night to tomorrow.

Flies stand guard at the storage;
they make the air around humid.

Giant footprints leave a well behind;
tongues lap the first water of the year.

The fear of death is not there anymore;
the sick are happy without medication.

The sugar coating of the tongue remains;
there is sweetness left of the bitter life.

The clothesline is in the air, I am flying
a kite with broken wings, tail torn off.

The wind is blowing; my heart holds
fast to the hope of coming down calm.

II

If you meet people walking backwards,
do you run to overtake them or retreat?

There is no map of the future without smudges;
to read the roads you need an outfit of faith.

If the iroko grew roots up and leaves down,
would it still be the great conclave of spirits?

I once saw a man dead, standing, chalk in hand;
it was not long before a shrine sprang up there –

shadows of afterlife dance with the womenfolk;
the men, gin-drunk, stuck to their waists in mud.

In the farms the workers pick up songs of the dead,
there has been no voice as sweet as the stilled singer's;

the spirits replenish their energy with fanciful songs,
they took them away but their loud echoes persist.

In the absence of men chimpanzees court beauties;
the world hesitates for lack of trust in fine words –

those walking backwards are seeking those running
to a front without a future in their misted faith;

it is not walking or dancing that will save the world.
There are shadows whose bodies can never be seen.

III

Daddy Showkey is having a concert.
Dancing are orphans and their resurrected mothers.

If you see my Papa hosanna
give him this fish eye to eat hosanna

he turned a blind eye on my sufferings hosanna
he demands sacrifice twofold my earnings hosanna

Daddy Showkey thrusts his behind backward
and gracefully digs his trademark steps forward.

Dancing to his cue are orphans and their mothers,
the concert thrice postponed because of forecast

now rain still beats dancers and singers;
hands in the air they freeze on the spot.

If you see my Papa hosanna
bring him to court for the torture in the compound hosanna

if he lost his mother he would meet her hosanna
let him tell her what I am telling mine hosanna

King of fools

King of fools, they hail the lone one;
they wear him a cellophane robe
and everybody claps at his distinction.

He follows the queue orderly,
gets overtaken by everybody else
and, left behind, laughs at himself.

He bows not to extortion at roadblocks
set up by barbarous police who butt him
to bleed profusely for being law-abiding.

He allows others to have their share
and to leave his, only for his portion
to be wiped out before his patient turn.

He stands upright in the crooked lane –
they keep a safe distance from him
they believe is deviant and depraved.

He tells the only truth in the republic,
faces jeers and taunts across the land;
the jury of liars gives him a life sentence.

In the nation jinxed with insolvency,
he is the sacrifice and its carrier.
King of fools, they hail the lone one.

We know why

We know why the grazing cow allows
the egret, without challenge, to pick
its back and hop from hump to hind.

Now is the season of foraging forays
for green foliage before another season
scorches the earth and starts famine

that must send cows out on a long trail
to fight over another country's food
and live consumed by daily prayers.

Refugees on the move, death poaches fast –
limbs worn out by sole-searing sand dunes;
crossing guarded frontiers exacts a high toll.

The savannah is currently a kind country;
it provides water troughs and fresh grass –
the abundance cannot be taken for granted.

There is no time now to scratch burning itches
with ticks digging their teeth all over the body
and neither arm stretches far to pull them out.

Let the ticks boast of lifting a heavyweight
with their teeth; let them swell with pride
because of the feast they make of the cow.

The cow's tail lashes out at flies; fixated,
it cannot stretch out to reach everywhere
on the back that undulates hill and valley.

As for the crescent horn, a shield and spear
against bigger fighters, it gores; but here
no buffalo or rhino to test stabbing power.

Let the cow moo and not give up a second
because of troublemakers that are so tiny
they cannot arrest it in this kind country.

So let the egrets feed on the foraging ticks,
mercifully rid the cow of a pestilent crowd;
let them enjoy this immunity, a godsend.

Nomads learn to be generous to each other
as today's abundance is tomorrow's dearth
and every migration invites death to poach.

The small live on the big, servants on lords
even when they devour smaller irritants –
the collective spirit of the savannah prevails

to keep all alive in the season of abundance
except rinderpest breaks out and God help all;
scrounging life laid waste for vultures' feast.

The grazing cow allows the egret,
without challenge, to pick its back and hop
from hump to hind. We know why.

Able-bodies blues

A cripple travelled
waterways in a canoe

and like everyone had
to sit the entire route.

He journeyed on land
riding an elephant like

others saving soles;
nobody atop was taller.

An aircraft flew him
over ranges of mountains

that yielded to no climbers.
He did not stand out

among upright ones
envious of his moving

so fast and his easy life
until they discovered

his two shrivelled legs
and sighed in disbelief.

The mass hunt

Let's drive them into their holes:
ants that condemn our feet for murder

locusts that consume our greens
crickets that perforate our plots

rats that bite our soles in deep sleep
fowls that ambush us with droppings

fish that diminish our water resources
snakes that plant their teeth in the field

vegetables that throw up the palate's good taste
mushrooms that sell poison in the farmers' market

trees that flaunt scarecrows before our eyes
children that contest seniority with parents

women that do not love with their hearts
men that suffocate with their animal capers

gods that knock worshippers' heads together
let's drive them all into their holes

and what bigger holes will be left
to swallow survivors of the mass hunt!

Remembering

(for Ezekiel Okpan)

The day the farmer lost all his harvest to locusts
the day the herdsman lost all his cows to rinderpest

the day the fisherman lost his boat and nets to a storm
the day there was a total eclipse of the sun

the day fire left dry leaves to burn out green ones
the day water failed to quench the burning thirst

the day the wind refused to blow away smothering fumes
the day the earth opened a bottomless pit to another world

the day the muse thrashed the minstrel
the day the minstrel was struck dumb

the day the goat refused to eat yam leaves
the day the parrot refused to eat corn

the day the drums refused to beat for the dancer
the day the iroko was struck down by lightning

the day erased from the memory of celebrations
the day gone down without a record of its hours

the day all the gates closed to the fugitive
the day the crossroads refused its sacrifice

the day all the alarms refused to go off
the day the clear-eyed guide lost his vision

the day the boneless beast opened its mouth
to swallow an entire man like sautéed crayfish

that was the day of the summer solstice when in Jerusalem my best friend died in Sapele.

(Hawthornden Castle. June 21, 2004)

To the janjaweed

May the fire you spread gleefully this way
scorch you and your family at the other end

may your patrons in government corridors
become dead vultures to the entire world

may the horses you ride to sack villages
throw you into vainglorious days

may the identity you hide now in scarves
be stripped by the Maker when you need cover

may those you chase out of life in these raids
turn round to pursue you out of the next life

may your sway over darkness strangle you
and day reduce you to the lowest vermin

may you escape justice of Khartoum's courts
and be condemned forever in a higher trial

may those you kill to seize their property
deny you the ultimate refuge of peace

may djinns you invoke in your despoliation
testify against you in the final judgment

may you be victim of your blood thirst
and wander without relief from paradise

may the fire seeds you sow in Darfur
consume you and your damned bands . . .

Homes

They built two houses for my convenience.
I paid for one with cash; the other mortgaged.

I leave the storey house for the vinyl bungalow
and back again to where I spurned for the other –

the dirt and odours of one compete for distaste
with the fragility and volatility of the other.

My father built his own earthen house
from floor to roof with clay and wood –

he was so secure in it that only farm work
and necessary social obligations took him out

and rumours went round that my mother so charmed him
that he remained at home to prattle about her all the time.

But I made nothing of my two elegant houses;
both contracted out from start to finish.

Instead of being contented with one house
as Father's on inherited family land

my two plots were bought from speculators;
both unrelated to me in blood and custom.

I claim two residencies separated by deep water
and my property in both places leased to me.

Each though is my home but not home enough
despite the uplifting gadgets and decorations.

I run out of either one when a crisis flares;
unlike my father who prepared to die in his –

I am at heart a refugee at either home;
gunshots outside keep me homebound.

My children live in both homes only in name
as they are always chased out by nightmares.

So when the parrot has crossed the sea and alights,
the song has risen and fallen into obdurate silence

the archer sun has exhausted its arrows and withdraws,
the son in youth and age has begotten sons to bear sons

none of the two houses will be home
to whom the whole world is not big enough

but somewhere outside, raised for the occasion
with competing songs and flowers in sunlight,

is the true home, the house of words, always there
and open to the entire world to claim in song . . .

Glossary

Amreghe: The poet's grandmother.

Apiapia: Bird of the falcon family that cries *pia pia* as it flies.

Daddy Showkey: Niger Delta-born musician based in Ajegunle, Lagos, who sings about the plight of the downtrodden.

Darfur: Large region of western Sudan where Arab militias (the Janjaweed), supported by the government in Khartoum, have been committing acts of unspeakable inhumanity against blacks of the area.

Djenné: Ancient city in Mali at the Niger River bend.

Egbesu Boys: Young fighters struggling for resource control in the oil-rich Bayelsa State.

Escravos: Oil-loading port for super-tankers in Nigeria's Delta State. Apparently the Portuguese gave the place the name because it was a slave-exporting port.

Futa Djalon: The area around the source of the River Niger in Guinea.

Goat song: Also "song of a goat"; originating from the Greek; a lament, a tragic song. Here it represents a song of anguish and complaint.

Godwin, Boyi, and Obatavwe: Childhood friends of the poet.

Hawthornden Castle: Near Edinburgh, Scotland.

Ifri: The Izon equivalent of the Urhobo Ivwri, god of restitution and revenge.

Mowoe: Great personality of the late 1940s who brought unity to the Urhobo group.

Ogidigbo: Legendary Urhobo warrior.

Omoja: A stream by Okuribada, the now-abandoned village, where the poet was raised by his grandmother.

Ozidi: Legendary Izon warrior.

Rinderpest: Viral infection that kills cows.

Steepletop: The Millay Colony for the Arts, near Austerlitz, Upstate New York.

Sundiata: Great emperor of ancient Mali, the subject of epic songs.

Kraftgriots

Also in the series (POETRY) *continued*

Ebi Yeibo: *Maiden Lines* (2004)
Barine Ngaage: *Rhythms of Crisis* (2004)
Funso Aiyejina: *I, The Supreme & Other Poems* (2004)
'Lere Oladitan: *Boolekaja: Lagos Poems 1* (2005)
Seyi Adigun: *Bard on the Shore* (2005)
Famous Dakolo: *A Letter to Flora* (2005)
Olawale Durojaiye: *An African Night* (2005)
g'ebinyŏ ogbowei: *let the honey run & other poems* (2005)
Joe Ushie: *Popular Stand & Other Poems* (2005)
Gbemisola Adeoti: *Naked Soles* (2005)
Aj. Dagga Tolar: *This Country is not a Poem* (2005)
Tunde Adeniran: *Labyrinthine Ways* (2006)
Sophia Obi: *Tears in a Basket* (2006)
Tonyo Biriabebe: *Undercurrents* (2006)
Ademola O. Dasylva: *Songs of Odamolugbe* (2006), winner, 2006 ANA/Cadbury
    poetry prize
George Ehusani: *Flames of Truth* (2006)
Abubakar Gimba: *This Land of Ours* (2006)
G. 'Ebinyo Ogbowei: *the heedless ballot box* (2006)
Hyginus Ekwuazi: *Love Apart* (2006), winner, 2007 ANA/NDDC Gabriel Okara
    poetry prize and winner, 2007 ANA/Cadbury poetry prize
Abubakar Gimba: *Inner Rumblings* (2006)
Albert Otto: *Letters from the Earth* (2007)
Aj. Dagga Tolar: *Darkwaters Drunkard* (2007)
Idris Okpanachi: *The Eaters of the Living* (2007), winner, 2008 ANA/Cadbury
    poetry prize
Tubal-Cain: *Mystery in Our Stream* (2007), winner, 2006 ANA/NDDC Gabriel
    Okara poetry prize
John Iwuh: *Ashes & Daydreams* (2007)
Sola Owonibi: *Chants to the Ancestors* (2007)
Adewale Aderinale: *The Authentic* (2007)
Ebi Yeibo: *The Forbidden Tongue* (2007)
Doutimi Kpakiama: *Salute to our Mangrove Giants* (2008)
Halima M. Usman: *Spellbound* (2008)
Hyginus Ekwuazi: *Dawn Into Moonlight: All Around Me Dawning* (2008), winner,
    2008 ANA/NDDC Gabriel Okara poetry prize
Ismail Bala Garba & Abdullahi Ismaila (eds.): *Pyramids: An Anthology of Poems
    from Northern Nigeria* (2008)
Denja Abdullahi: *Abuja Nunyi (This is Abuja)* (2008)
Japhet Adeneye: *Poems for Teenagers* (2008)
Seyi Hodonu: *A Tale of Two in Time (Letters to Susan)* (2008)
Ibukun Babarinde: *Running Splash of Rust and Gold* (2008)
Chris Ngozi Nkoro: *Trails of a Distance* (2008)

67

Tunde Adeniran: *Beyond Finalities* (2008)
Abba Abdulkareem: *A Bard's Balderdash* (2008)
Ifeanyi D. Ogbonnaya: *... And Pigs Shall Become House Cleaners* (2008)
g'ebinyŏ ogbowei: *the town crier's song* (2009)
g'ebinyŏ ogbowei: *song of a dying river* (2009)
Sophia Obi-Apoko: *Floating Snags* (2009)
Akachi Adimora-Ezeigbo: *Heart Songs* (2009), winner, 2009 ANA/Cadbury poetry prize
Hyginus Ekwuazi: *The Monkey's Eyes* (2009)
Seyi Adigun: *Prayer for the Mwalimu* (2009)
Faith A. Brown: *Endless Season* (2009)
B.M. Dzukogi: *Midnight Lamp* (2009)
B.M. Dzukogi: *These Last Tears* (2009)
Chimezie Ezechukwu: *The Nightingale* (2009)
Ummi Kaltume Abdullahi: *Tiny Fingers* (2009)
Ismaila Bala & Ahmed Maiwada (eds.): *Fireflies: An Anthology of New Nigerian Poetry* (2009)
Eugenia Abu: *Don't Look at Me Like That* (2009)
Data Osa Don-Pedro: *You Are Gold and Other Poems* (2009)
Sam Omatseye: *Mandela's Bones and Other Poems* (2009)
Sam Omatseye: *Dear Baby Ramatu* (2009)
C.O. Iyimoga: *Fragments in the Air* (2010)
Bose Ayeni-Tsevende: *Streams* (2010)
Seyi Hodonu: *Songs from My Mother's Heart (2010)*, winner ANA/NDDC Gabriel Okara poetry prize, 2010
Akachi Adimora-Ezeigbo: *Waiting for Dawn* (2010)
Hyginus Ekwuazi: *That Other Country* (2010), winner, ANA/Cadbury poetry prize, 2010
Emmanuel Frank-Opigo: *Masks and Facades* (2010)
Tosin Otitoju: *Comrade* (2010)
Arnold Udoka: *Poems Across Borders* (2010)
Arnold Udoka: *The Gods Are So Silent & Other Poems* (2010)
Abubakar Othman: *The Passions of Cupid* (2010)
Okinba Launko: *Dream-Seeker on Divining Chain* (2010)
'kufre ekanem: *the ant eaters* (2010)
McNezer Fasehun: *Ever Had a Dear Sister* (2010)
Baba S. Umar: *A Portrait of My People* (2010)
Gimba Kakanda: *Safari Pants* (2010)
Sam Omatseye: *Lion Wind & Other Poems* (2011)
Ify Omalicha: *Now that Dreams are Born* (2011)
Karo Okokoh: *Souls of a Troubadour* (2011)
Ada Onyebuenyi, Chris Ngozi Nkoro, Ebere Chukwu (eds): *Uto Nka: An Anthology of Literature for Fresh Voices* (2011)
Mabel Osakwe: *Desert Songs of Bloom* (2011)
Pious Okoro: *Vultures of Fortune & Other Poems* (2011)
Godwin Yina: *Clouds of Sorrows* (2011)
Nnimmo Bassey: *I Will Not Dance to Your Beat* (2011)
Denja Abdullahi: *A Thousand Years of Thirst* (2011)
Enoch Ojotisa: *Commoner's Speech* (2011)
Rowland Timi Kpakiama: *Bees and Beetles* (2011)

Lawrence Ogbo Ugwuanyi: *Let Them Not Run* (2011)
Saddiq M. Dzukogi: *Canvas* (2011)
Arnold Udoka: *Running with My Rivers* (2011)
Olusanya Bamidele: *Erased Without a Trace* (2011)
Olufolake Jegede: *Treasure Pods* (2012)
Karo Okokoh: *Songs of a Griot* (2012), winner. ANA/NDDC Gabriel Okara poetry prize, 2012
Musa Idris Okpanachi: *From the Margins of Paradise* (2012)
John Martins Agba: *The Fiend and Other Poems* (2012)
Sunnie Ododo: *Broken Pitchers* (2012)
'Kunmi Adeoti: *Epileptic City* (2012)
Ibiwari Ikiriko: *Oily Tears of the Delta* (2012)
Bala Dalhatu: *Moonlights* (2012)
Karo Okokoh: *Manna for the Mind* (2012)
Chika O. Agbo: *The Fury of the Gods* (2012)
Emmanuel C. S. Ojukwu: *Beneath the Sagging Roof* (2012)
Amirikpa Oyigbenu: *Cascades and Flakes* (2012)
Ebi Yeibo: *Shadows of the Setting Sun* (2012)
Chikaoha Agoha: *Shreds of Thunder* (2012)
Mark Okorie: *Terror Verses* (2012)
Clemmy Igwebike-Ossi: *Daisies in the Desert* (2012)
Idris Amali: *Back Again (At the Foothills of Greed)* (2012)
A.N. Akwanya: *Visitant on Tiptoe* (2012)
Akachi Adimora-Ezeigbo: *Dancing Masks* (2013)
Chinazo-Bertrand Okeomah: *Furnace of Passion* (2013)
g'ebinyō ogbowei: *marsh boy and other poems* (2013)
Ifeoma Chinwuba: *African Romance* (2013)
Remi Raji: *Sea of my Mind* (2013)
Francis Odinya: *Never Cry Again in Babylon* (2013)
Immanuel Unekwuojo Ogu: *Musings of a Pilgrim* (2013)
Khabyr Fasasi: *Tongues of Warning* (2013)
J.C.P. Christopher: *Salient Whispers* (2014)
Paul T. Liam: *Saint Sha'ade and other poems* (2014)
Joy Nwiyi: *Burning Bottom* (2014)
R. Adebayo Lawal: *Melodreams* (2014)
R. Adebayo Lawal: *Music of the Muezzin* (2014)
Idris Amali: *Efeega: War of Ants* (2014)
Samuel Onungwe: *Tantrums of a King* (2014)
Bizuum G. Yadok: *Echoes of the Plateau* (2014)
Abubakar Othman: *Bloodstreams in the Desert* (2014)
rome aboh: *a torrent of terror* (2014)
Udenta O. Udenta: *37 Seasons Before the Tornado* (2015)
Magnus Abraham-Dukuma: *Dreams from the Creek* (2015)
Christian Otobotekere: *The Sailor's Son 1* (2015)

Printed in the United States
By Bookmasters